Stranger in Town

New and Selected Poems

Stranger in Town
New and Selected Poems

Ron McFarland

Confluence Press
Lewiston, Idaho

Acknowledgments

Poems in this collection first appeared in the following magazines and periodicals and have on a few occasions been slightly altered since their original appearance in print. The editors and publishers of the following magazines gave my poems their first chance, and I greatly appreciate their confidence: *Redneck Review of Literature, Weber Studies, Trestle Creek Review, Wind, Talking River Review, The New Taste, The Temple, Dickinson Review, Independent Voice, Apocalypse, Urbanus, Sport Literate, South Coast Poetry Journal, Hemingway Review, Tar River Poetry, Rockhurst Review, Heartbeat, Hampden-Sydney Poetry Review, Portland Review, Birmingham Poetry Review, Yarrow, Tomorrow, Midwest Quarterly, Kinesis, Hiram Poetry Review, Slow Dancer, Excursus, Willow Springs, Cumberland Poetry Review, Threepenny Review, Owen Wister Review, Black Bear Review, Spitball, North Dakota Quarterly, Crab Creek Review, Salt Fork Review, Rattapallax.*

Publication of Confluence Press books is made possible, in part, by the generosity of the Idaho Commission on the Arts, Lewis-Clark State College, and Washington State University.

www.confluencepress.com

Cover art by Mel McCuddin
Cover and text design by John K. Wilper

FIRST EDITION
10 9 8 7 6 5 4 3 2 1

Library of Congress Control Number: 00-131798
ISBN: 1-881090-38-8

Published by:
Confluence Press, Inc.
Lewis-Clark State College
500 Eighth Avenue
Lewiston, ID 83501
(208) 799-2336

Distributed by:
Midpoint Trade Books
1263 Southwest Boulevard
Kansas City, KS 66103
(913) 831-2233
Fax (913) 362-7401

For my parents

Earl A. McFarland
Mary Maxine Stullenburger McFarland

CONTENTS

I. Stranger in Town: New Poems

II. Certain Women (1977)

III. Composting at Forty (1984)

IV. The Haunting Familiarity of Things (1993)

IV. Ballgloves (2000)

"Which of us is not forever a stranger and alone?"

—Thomas Wolfe
Look Homeward, Angel!

I. Stranger in Town: New Poems

At the Museum of Lost Toys

Clay marbles someone's grandfather
shot across the ring in 1914
line up by size and color
waiting for some boy's thumb to
flick them out of this glass case
back into the world of dust and sun.

Here an exquisite set of jacks
scatters on a field of green velvet
just right for threesies.
The girl with short brown hair
sweeps them up with her mind,
believing they want out.

Stiffly tilted, six bright tops
lie on their sides spun out
by time and the shifting laws
of physics. Building a great pool
of inertial and potential energy,
they poise for kinetic whips.

Two boys press against the glass
protected battleground where the Iron
Duke wins again. In the next display
the Germans die at Kursk, SS Grenadiers
left in leaden sprawl, dead but bloodless.
War, the boys must think, is just like that.

In this silent museum porcelain dolls
stare mutely into the future as if
catatonic in their memories of love.
This was what it was like to be held,
caressed. The bride doll with real
human hair recalls the comb and brush,

genuine ivory. The black doll,
eyes bulging, reaches out for this
new justice the world brags about.
The world's first talking doll
speaks French, but her message is
universal: "Maman," she says. "Mama."

The Apology

That night the moon burned orange
from the smoke of forest fires,
or almost gold, he had to say,
something thick with value
in exchange for what he knew
he should have said, or rather
what he shouldn't have shouted
a couple of hours before.

Now in the half-moon dark
his father stood beside him
awaiting the apology
he couldn't say at night any more
than in broad daylight. In silence
the words gathered and the moon
drifted in the smoke between them.

Now his father would have to say
something about how long the summer was,
how dry, about the early harvest,
low wheat prices once again,
about the baseball strike, or
anything else to set the world right.

Fantaisie Adolescente

She mowed the lawn off and on
all day, not the way her father
wanted it, but the job would get done.

She liked the way her father
always found a single strip uncut,
then mowed it down with a vengeance,

and the way he always overlooked
how she trimmed the marigolds,
peonies and sprawling iris blades.

If she saved up every dollar
she could buy a twenty year-old car
in about ten years, by which time

she would be twenty-five years old.
Mike would've joined the Navy and married
somebody else. She stopped for a Coke.

She called Cassie, and Cassie said
be sure to phone Tina, who said
phone Jennifer, which she did.

She liked the way her father
complained over gin and tonic
about all the jerks at the office.

Now she was starving but there was
never anything to eat because
her mother hated her. Definitely.

On television this great looking boy
complained that his girlfriend dressed
like a slut. She had to agree, he

definitely deserved better, someone
like herself for example. Why were
all the guys in this town so dumb?

What happened to all the daylight? Where
had it gone? How could she mow now?
What would her father say when he got home?

The Curiosity

Children, curious about death,
touch flattened squirrels, inter sparrows
with full military honors.
Even a rhinoceros beetle
stiff with rigor mortis under the Florida sun,
swarmed with ravenous ants,
draws their rapt attention,
stirs their awareness that something
should be done, the solemn sarcophagus
of a peanut butter jar,
a few sprigs of grass
in case it comes back to life hereafter.

All good pets go to heaven, except
     goldfish,
          which spiral
               walleyed and cold
down the toilet, through the sewer,
along the Mississippi and out to sea,
perhaps the Sea of Eternity.
Death seems to be one of those places.

At what age do children come to
distrust the dead, to regard them warily,
to disown them, even to
resent their sudden departure?
The dead become unwanted food
neglected on their plates,
swept under bread crusts, objects
of strange allergies.
Force the children and they turn away,
angry, bolt from the table.
They will go to bed without supper,
sulking, weeping in anguish
at the clear injustice of their fathers.
They would rather starve
than eat that food.

Taking Fire

That boy who saw his dad
struck dead by lightning
became a pyromaniac, you said,
felt fires dancing in his head
for years and had to put them
out the only way he could.

That boy became the torch of God
flaming first in dark hearts
of old barns and brittle fields,
and then wherever light was needed.
He knew he was the lantern
scorching out the truth
wherever it lurked, always hidden:
volatile corners of the paint store,
the old furniture outlet,
of course the school.

That boy found love in the red
embers, in the wild glow of
firemen's faces, the crazy fear
of innocent bystanders. Let's say
they never caught him, say
he grew old in the ashes
of his own creations, a little odd
perhaps, but mostly normal,
knowing you cannot burn God.

Wheatspill

Not golden really, tan and yellow
with a splash of light,
a spray of grain washes the highway
in a bright wave.

The truck we read about last night,
heeled into the ditch,
is long since hauled away
in a flicker of red and white.

The body of the boy who played
defensive tackle for the Bulldogs
lies in a funeral home he never knew
existed, awaiting the tears

of cheerleaders, classmates,
the girl he never noticed
who sat beside him in math
crying hardest of all.

The wheatspill brightens the road,
what's left of green memories
scattered on dark gravel
birds and wind will gather up.

Van Gogh's Boots

Stumbling over his boots in the dark
made him feel like such a fool!
Who put them there, after all,
with their tongues hanging out?
Who could he blame but himself?
No wife, no children, not even
an embittered lover to scold
for these old hobnailed clodhoppers.

They came from his own dumb feet
that rambled around all day
scarcely missing a step.
But here he was almost ready for bed
nearly falling over these empty husks
of himself that ran full tilt
across the yard with him,
that kicked a pine cone down the walk,
that skipped upstairs and down,
that strolled from here to there
and back again as usual and then

got taken off and tossed aside
like an idle thought.
So he deserved this in a way,
clumsy slob, to be almost
assassinated by his own sad boots.

Edgar Allan Poe Goes Fishing
(June 3, 1841)

This is after he has been expelled from West Point,
and after marrying his fourteen or fifteen year-old cousin,
and one year after *Tales of the Grotesque and Arabesque.*
He is thirty-one and living in Philadelphia,
and sniping at Longfellow, and fishing the Delaware
from the shore just north of town.

The weather is warm and muggy, and the fishing is bad,
and he never liked fishing anyway, but Virginia
wanted him out of the house. He catches
two or three measly bluegill, snaps his pole
on a big carp, which makes him think of
John Greenleaf Whittier, which makes him sad.

The two fish stiffen in a pail of tepid water,
their flat, glossy eyes wide open with accusation,
shocked to see how cold-blooded he can be.
They have not read "Ligeia," his personal favorite,
have no idea what's on his mind. They have not even read
"The Fall of the House of Usher." It was not assigned.

Poe is wondering whether they would make good bait,
not the fish themselves, of course, and not a strip
cut from their belly or sides, but their eyes,
their large, wild, black-on-amber eyes.

Walt Whitman Meets a Nice Girl

(Washington, D.C., September 1863)

She was not yet seventeen but full of zeal
for doing her part, a patriot fresh to the city
from the farm in Ohio, Belmont County
she said, as if he should know
just where that was. He was a poet,
wasn't he? No, she had not read his book.

He was almost forty-four and full of joy
and sorrow and broken wisdom, a city
fellow from Brooklyn he said,
as if she should know that
even though she had so far
wasted her life reading Longfellow.

She loved *Evangeline*. He smiled
indulgently, avuncular, she was so young,
her mind unfreighted with life
until she witnessed her first amputation.
Then she fainted while he wiped sweat
and tears from the dying soldier's eyes.

After a long day of anguish they met
under a live oak and he recited a poem
about Louisiana and she liked it,
gripped his hands until his fingers hurt.
Her brother was with Sherman
somewhere in Tennessee or Georgia.

Her mother was in Heaven. They were
Presbyterians and she thought her father
would like him, but he disagreed
politely. He was a gentleman and smart,
but what did he, of all men,
know about a lonely girl's heart?

Altercation

Of course he said nothing about it to Elsie,
but to a friend he wrote of two cases of Scotch,
unstringing a brass monkey, and a huge cloud
dancing with señoritas from Habana
clicking their castanets in the balmy air.
He and the judge and Hem fishing and drinking
at Long Key, pretending to be good ol' boys.

They "disagreed on certain things" and they
were "pretty well lit." This was before the war,
1936, just before *To Have and Have Not*,
and no one insulted Papa Hemingway and
got away with it. You can imagine that
roundhouse right winging in from somewhere
out in the Gulf of Mexico square into his eye,
and him knocked staggering flat on his derriere
two or three times, a big guy but soft
and out of shape and drunk as a skunk
and the humid air heavy with key lime blossoms
or night blooming cereus if in season.

He lumbers to his feet and throws a wild punch
drawn from some radio broadcast of Jack Dempsey
cracking into the author's jaw, but what cracks
is his own hand. Later he said he laughed it off,
said he never read much fiction anyway, said
Hemingway had the makings of a fine poet.

Hemingway in Africa: The Untold Story

During his first trip to the Serengeti
Hemingway killed more than thirty
wild animals, including three lions,
and one uncelebrated parakeet
belonging to the only woman he ever met
but never wrote or talked about.
She must have betrayed him
and one sultry afternoon,
buoyed on Beefeater's,
he popped open the wicker cage
and watched the bird's powder blue flight
to the lower limb of a camphor tree.
He grinned, but not maliciously,
knowing she would not speak to him again.
She must have been beautiful,
the best of the lot, perhaps
more gorgeous than The Kraut herself
to force him to lift up
his elephant gun, his short, ugly,
shockingly big-bored .505 Gibbs,
straight out of the pages of "The Short,
Happy Life of Francis Macomber,"
and blow that parakeet to smithereens.

Dancing Emily Dickinson

To dance Emily Dickinson move
slowly, then slower, then
not at all.
Move like shadows in slanted light
turning vivid as wild nights
lived only in dream.
Move in whiteness, not as in
innocence, not as in
virginity, not
as in light,
but as in the clouded ice of death.
Try to think of your father
if you did not like him,
but only loved him as the Bible
commands.
Try to think of God.
Dance the way God would dance
if he were a lonely woman
living in Amherst,
Massachusetts,
in the middle of the nineteenth
century, not
thinking about heading west.

Backing Down

Once in the blink of an eye
a yellow-streaked pine siskin
flickered into the brush
where I thought a bear might be.
That day I was loaded for deer,
but I never have wanted to see
either a deer or a bear
slip into my open sights,
so I was prepared to fire
straight through the duff and soil
to spare whatever was there.

They say you can smell a bear,
but I smelled nothing that day
except for the pungent pine
stinging the autumn air.
Instead of a husky cough
I heard a wheezy buzz,
and yet I knew it was there,
a few steps into the dark,
ready to whisper death
into my stuttering ears.

I stood there staring, afraid,
awaiting the huff and charge,
the razor slash of its claws,
its foul breath burning my face.
I took a big step back
as one bird called to another,
a flutter of olive and gray
sending my thumb to the safety.
I stepped back down that trail,
my rifle tense in my hands,
and never looked behind
but trusted the quick pine siskins
to cover my nervous retreat.

Baking Pies

While I climbed the sprawling green
pie apple tree, famous for its small
wormy fruit, my never-to-be-married
Great Aunt Estelle held forth in the kitchen
with her fork, cutting Crisco into the flour
and shouting over her deafness at my mother.

Didn't my Great Aunt Estelle own the best
Victorian house in Barnesville, Ohio?
Why was my fearless mother so afraid of her,
my father's favorite aunt, who could
take her teeth out with the tip of her tongue?
Her younger half-brother wore a marvelous
glass eye he said he could take out any time
and shoot like a marble, called it his taw
and said he'd take me on whenever,
but he only played for keeps.

While the pie baked, my Great Aunt Estelle,
a lousy cook, even the ubiquitous all-American
apple pie defied her, would play dominoes,
beating me incessantly, sending my tremulous
fingers dancing back to the bone-yard
among the treacherous ivory rectangles.
They were real ivory, she once said, carved
from the tusks of African elephants.
"Don't be afraid," she would say, "just play.
You can learn a lot from losing."

And that night my mother would cry
all the short ride home, my father saying
softly, it's all right, everything's okay,
a warm apple pie on her lap.

Family History

Here is my grandfather
crawling hand over hand
through the coal black
world of Mark Hanna,
so dark he cannot
read his own name
tattooed in blue on his
forearm. Outside my uncle
squats apart from the adults
as close to the shaft
as the somber rescuers
and silent miners allow.

When my grandfather
crawls into the light,
he surfaces in Florida
at the gas station
on Merritt Island
where the sun is so bright
his tattoo begins to fade.
"It don't matter," he says,
"I know who I am by now."
My uncle, home from Korea,
learns how to do a lube job,
pump gas, change oil.

Here is my grandfather
mowing the lawn in August
in the middle of the day
when he should know better.
What's he doing on that ladder

at his age? "Mary," he calls,
my grandmother, "I don't
feel so good." My uncle
looks for a pulse below
that useless blue tattoo,
my grandfather's arm
fading under the sun.

Public Enemies

Something pinged at National Airport
in Washington, D.C., so there I stood
arms outstretched like a felon
or secular Christ crucified in neon
nakedness as the black security cop
with a friendly professional grin
ran his electric baton over my
potentially murderous body.
I could feel the eyes of strangers
scan me with dread suspicion.
Mothers pulled their children aside.
They could tell I was the type.

The next afternoon in Georgetown
strolling innocently down the towpath
of the old C&O canal where a dozen
mallards, the males flashing neon-
green heads, stirred up mud
littered with beer cans and plastic,
I came upon one of the homeless,
black man with arms outstretched
directing himself a-cappella.
They say it's best to avoid eye contact.
I felt for my trusty pocketknife.
He was the type. I could tell.

The Grammar of Memoir

Often I try to think of myself
as something more than a pronoun,
a noun for instance, that of which
a pronoun takes the place,
man, for example, poet perhaps,
angler, athlete, husband, father,
son and brother, poker player,
lover extraordinaire if I may be so
adjectival for a moment, or
maybe the jerk who flipped you
off at the intersection of
Fourth and Participle. But
just once I'd like to pass myself
off as a verb, and not a verb
of being but something, you know,
wildly transitive, no auxiliaries,
no adverbs to litter my pure act:
love, hate, weep, kill, kiss, and die.

Sunset 1996: Driving Westward

Driving straight into the dying light
westward through Montana
somewhere after Billings, the sun
burning furiously
as if to spite the darkness,
we shift our gaze away from the glare
into the substantial sagebrush.

Vision operates by tangents,
taking an angle on road signs offering
unlimited velocity,
advertisements for fresh prairie oysters,
franchised familiarity of name-brand
motels ahead. We consider stopping
for the night in Missoula.

Averting our eyes from the bright pain,
we squint, skewing the sun visors
left and right without success.
By the time we creep over the Divide
the sun has burned out,
leaving us cold, confused
in a solar system devoid of messages.

From the radio, quick with static
comes news of a boy in Idaho,
fifteen years old and dying of meningitis.
They amputated both legs
just below the knees that played
football last year for Timberline.
We cannot turn it off in time.

We try not to think of him
sitting on the icy aluminum bench
dreaming of the next season.
Neither of us says a word to Jon,
our almost sixteen defensive back,
silent behind us, trying to find
the right slant on things.

My Name is Ronda

Ronda's note in our motel room tells us she's
responsible, a good girl who will not steal
our brand new Nikon, even if we leave it in
plain sight.
      "Every item," the note reads,
"must be accounted for by me. Placed in this
room are: 3 washcloths, 3 hand towels, 3
bath towels, 1 bath mat."
      We feel grateful
for the bureaucratic sanction of the passive
voice. "Thank you," she says, "for the oppor-
tunity to serve you.
      Thank you for staying
with us!!!" Three exclamation marks to balance
the towels and washcloths. She's so grateful
we almost fail to be offended by her suspi-
cious nature.
      But my dear wife never misses
such slights. "Who does she think she is?"
she demands, slipping a hand towel into her
unscrupulous suitcase.

Pocatello Decor

A few miles outside Pocatello, Idaho,
past the gray plumes of phosphate plants
it's easy to see how potato skins get their color,
one with the earth as they are,
and their flat starchy American flavor.
The faded green of sagebrush seems about right,
the green of sweet corn out of place,
the stuff of dreams
and lines of irrigation pipe on wheels.

At Elmer's, across from the university,
the walls are hung with the Swiss alps
as if the Tetons were not enough.
Thick bright polymers replicate the Matterhorn
as a local myth of cozy chalets
without potatoes and sugar beets.
The artist started with massive frames,
baroque and antique gold,
and filled them up with landscapes
worthy of such impressive edges.

The owner says his mother read Byron
and painted these odd romances
of what Idaho should have been.
The owner would prefer the Sawtooths
or a bull elk bugling beside the Big Lost River.
A few miles outside town you can
pull off the interstate and see
wagon ruts from the old Oregon Trail.

Native

From a distance they could be mountain goats
or small white boulders lined up in the sun
until one of them steps away, and then . . . .
Investigating close, you see its tongue
unfolded, goofy from its mouth, and it only
looks like what it is, hair matted, not
exactly alabaster, scarcely white in fact.

Moving closer, thinking to touch the thing
because everyone insists, no other reason
being pertinent, you may perhaps detect
the quick shifting of indigenous ticks at home
and once in harmony with their host
as you, intruder, can never hope to be.

An Idaho Perspective

Back in '72 you could by God just about
make a living in the woods driving an 18-wheeler,
Silver Dome, Big Burn, Little Baldy, names on a map
some bunch of hippies found somewhere in San Francisco.
Next thing you know they're right out here
strung across the road in sleeping bags,
chained up to trees, slamming spikes
into any cedar worth putting a saw to.
One of them dumped a bag of sugar
into the tank of Jim Metsker's old D-8,
about two thousand dollars worth of damage
and him with three kids and a sick wife
and no insurance.
            Marge says they're hypocrites
like the ones in Luke that can see the sky and the sun
but don't know the time of day. "Like they don't sit
on wooden chairs," she says, "and write their nasty lies
on paper made of pulp with cedar pencils and on tables
made of walnut."
            This one little gal, dishwater blonde
but not too bad lookin' after they cleaned her up,
cute little thing, like Marge says, "*some*body's
daughter," pipes up in court, we gotta have perspective.
Per-*spec*-tive. The trees was here before Columbus,
she says, some of them anyways, and they got a right to live.
Says we oughta think of our grandchildren.
She's what—twenty? Hell, I'm sixty-two
and I got grandkids, got four of 'em,
two girls, two boys, and the boys are by God
going to be loggers if I have anything to say about it,
and them girls could by God do a lot worse
than marry loggers.

           Then this little gal from Pasadena
or wherever starts to carry on, gets real mad,
and you should of heard the words
come out of that sweet little mouth, and hell,
I've heard 'em all, two years in Korea with the 82nd
Airborne. Then suddenly she starts into cryin'.
You never seen the like. Marge looks like
her face is gonna fall off. Courtroom gets real quiet,
and all you can hear is this little gal
sobbing like there was no tomorrow.
                         I look down
at my hands, study the stub of my left little finger
and think of the day I wrenched it off setting choker
somewhere around Quartz Ridge. I think about
how the fishing used to be down on the South Fork
before the silt. Some days I got too good a memory
for my own good. But I'm lucky. I got a real
high tolerance for pain.

Stranger in Town

Being a stranger in town you head
straight for the wrong restaurant,
where the crab sandwich is something
fishy, the coffee is instant but cold,
and the pie was stamped out by machine
two months ago, then flash-frozen
in a faraway city, spirited here,
and microwaved for you, personally.

The waitress feels sorry for herself
because she dropped out of school,
because she lost her only boyfriend,
because all she ever gained in her life
was ten pounds last month, because
she cannot seem to lose this job.
But she feels even sorrier for you,
so she tells you the story of her life.

Stumbling into the night, your ears
ringing from her disaster, you search
for a bar, and sure enough you find
the wrong one. The music is not right,
the bourbon tastes like old nails,
and the bartender instantly hates you
because you remind him of his ex-wife's
new mate (they're rafting the Selway).

You have done all this before.
Your wife says you always do it.
Best not to spend the night here, but
skedaddle now, before High Noon
catches up with you about midnight.
You've seen that movie before.
Being a stranger in town you can
hardly wait to get out by sundown,
but it's always already too late.

Dangerous Weather

Last night the newscaster said wet snow,
said avalanches in the mountain passes,
said population would reach six billion
worldwide by the turn of the century
if you want to know what the real blizzard
is all about.
                   He looks like a nice guy,
just the way he's supposed to. That's why
they hired him, a broad friendly smile,
nut-brown well-groomed hair, comfortably forty
forever, your father in his prime, your
favorite uncle.
              He grins sympathetically
right through those passengers stranded
in airports, asleep on relentless benches
in bus terminals. He shakes his head
sadly at the old Chevrolet crumpled
under the semi. He wishes he could do
something about all this, but he can't
and it's not his fault.
                But he sees things.
He sees there are too many of us in this
stormy world. He sees in his monitor
how we keep getting in each other's way,
how we slide disastrously into each other
as if hitting patch after patch of black ice.

Local Woman Lucky

Kathleen Schmidt, age seventy-two
who lives about three miles out of town
on Clemmons Road, felt lucky
last Saturday morning right
up till quarter of twelve,
her husband of fifty-one years
puttering in the shop, muttering
in German the way he does when he's
happy being angry at how things fit,
dowels stabbed out at odd angles
from the coffee table for example,
grandkids chattering in the kitchen,
so out she went to pick nasturtiums,
orange and gold, she doesn't call them
yellow, just reached down beside
the climbing rose and got herself
struck by a rattler, a little fellow
maybe two feet long, and was amazed,
she said from her hospital bed,
how hard it hit on the back
of her left hand but she had the good
sense to take off her wedding band
right away, called out for Herman,
cursing over the power drill, German
profanity sounds pretty much the same,
she said, and rounded up the grandkids,
one of them climbing the apple tree by then
and the little one crying for a boost, and
cut out for the clinic over in Pomeroy,
getting there just in time, the nurse said,
or she'd have been out of luck.

Dropped Ball

The wide receiver eyes his hands
suspiciously, astonished.

Who gave him these hands,
if they are in fact his hands?

Which that brown elliptical inflation
spinning in the grass at his feet

makes him doubt. He holds them up
for the crowd to confirm the fact,

for his own mother to bear witness.
Yes, these were the fingers that

wiggled their way out of her womb,
she's embarrassed to say. She waves.

Miss Kite, his fifth grade teacher,
would recognize his handwriting.

His empty signature might even look
familiar to someone at the bank.

How could these pathetic fingers
have managed even to bait a hook?

The wide receiver slaps his hands
together. They punish each other.

He raises his hands over his helmet
in disbelief, dismay, surrender.

The Coming of the Light

This afternoon we gaze a few dull moths
resting flush against the living-room wall
as if in camouflage, confusing plaster
for the bark of our old apple trees.
Their wings held rooflike over their
fuzzy abdomens, waiting to spread out
into the incandescent death we have
switched on against the darkness.

In the garden we watched their murderous
flutter among the cabbages and corn,
strafed them with beige clouds of Rotenone
that would surely kill them, the label says.
It would kill us too, given the chance.

Their small relatives lurk in our closets
chewing Grandpa's Eisenhower jacket
into O.D. shreds, perforating Mom's best
tweed coat from nineteen sixty-six.
I once knew a boy who swallowed two
mothballs, about as much naphthalene
as anyone would care to eat in a lifetime.
He thought they were sugar-frosted filberts,
the kind of candy my great-aunt Sylvie
used to keep in crystal bowls for grown-ups.

He just threw up and survived,
the way kids do, but these pale, ghostlike
creatures stuck motionless against the wall,
these almost harmless nuisances, helpless
light-struck staggerings dazed in air,
will die deep in their fragility as we
sometimes dream of dying ourselves,
falling but coddled by hopes of heaven
and the coming assimilation of light.

The Poet's Crisis

The poet's daughter plays the bamboo flute,
his wife bakes fresh bread three days a week,
and his son paints watercolors, dances ballet,
and meditates the *I Ching*. In fact they all
meditate together, and they hate television
with Keatsian passion.
                    They prefer watching
the sun rise over a private corner of a lake
they call *their* lake, and naming the birds,
and picking up stones that might be arrowheads.
Nez Perce, Coeur d'Alene.
                  The poet's daughter
knows the scientific names of almost all
the butterflies. At twelve she has composed
a flute sonata for the lepidoptera.
                    Not to be
outdone, the poet's wife is writing a memoir
of her grandmother who graduated Radcliffe in '36
fluent in seven languages and translated
top secret documents for the O.S.S. during the war
before they all moved West, where her great
grandfather homesteaded at the turn of the century
and got himself
                murdered by a crazed farmer
whose land he'd bought for a song. The poet's
daughter is now composing that song,
                      and the son
has undertaken wildlife photography, develops his own
prints, dances weekends in Seattle, and has begun
to sell his work in Chicago.
                  Of course the poet
built their splendid house all by himself, plumbing,
wiring, the whole shebang, he likes to say. His next
book is runner-up for the Pulitzer, and for several days
he is so delighted that he becomes

                                    deeply depressed.
Even his wife's best seven-grained bread does not
bring him out of it. Even his daughter's award-winning
flute performance in Portland does not bring him around.
Even the news of his son's one-man show in Denver
leaves him disconsolate.
                          In the midst of his meditations
he finds himself thinking
                          of starting to smoke again.
He buys a pack of unfiltered Camels and throws it away.
He smuggles a bottle of Jack Daniels into the garage,
planning to drink alone and become an alcoholic,
but drops it like a Freudian slip.
                                    He cannot write.
If he believed in guns he would shoot himself,
but he keeps stumbling over his own integrity
or cowardice (he's not sure which), and then
there's the wife, the kids.
                          One day when he's burning
trash by the garden, reading Robert Bly's latest book,
he drops it into the fire. He almost gets to it before it
blackens.
                Perhaps it did not fall from his envious hands.
Perhaps he dropped it without a second thought.
He goes inside for another book, Adrienne Rich, a random
grab from the crammed shelf, and just like that the book
slips into the flame.
                          He does it again and again until
he feels happy, ecstatic in fact, standing outside himself
in a sudden, untranslatable burst of joy.

Sight Reading

Remember trying to tap your foot just right,
catching the change in tempo, counting out rests,
guessing how the composer meant it to sound?
Later on all of this amounted to something,
but right then it was frightening, to know
you might come in a beat too soon and blow it
for everyone. What did you learn from that?
Perhaps responsibility, or maybe when to hold back,
keep a low profile.
                        Remember how the fingering
confused you at times? You glanced right and left
to check which valves the others were pressing,
desperate to do it right. Suddenly three-quarter time
appeared on the sheet, and it might have been
Chinese for all you knew. You couldn't tell
a march from a waltz.
                        That and the emergence of
three flats out of nowhere taught you something
about dealing with panic. Those were the days when
good was not good enough, and only your conductor
knew for certain whether what was happening could be
considered anything like music.
                        That night you would
take the field and march up a storm, lifting your knees,
staying in step. You had "El Capitan" memorized
bar by bar, every sharp and flat. You would rate
superior, but you would always remember what
you learned that off-key afternoon watching your
conductor's red face drop an octave.

Your Children, The Kids

Consider the long anguish of children,
the all-day sucker
stuck in the back of the throat,
and suddenly, from out of a bad dream,
Great Aunt Estelle
leaps from the picnic table and grabs you
by your convulsive heels, your face
purpling black,
and thwacks you on the back until,
your hair trailing in the dirt, the candy
pops strawberry
from your throat and your life is saved
for another day.

Let's say your parents are thinking of that
episode from your past
when the call comes, the cool professional voice
of the highway patrol,
Sergeant Somebody-or-other, and you're okay
but the car is totaled and he sincerely hopes
they have insurance,
good insurance, he adds, as if to intimate
whose fault it obviously was, and what the hell
were you doing out there
on *that* road at *that* time of night driving
at *that* speed with *that* girl no parent
would approve of but don't worry,
she will be okay.

Well, thank God, at least you got a scholarship,
and that should get you out of their
rapidly graying hair
for at least four years, and then who knows,
maybe law school, or with luck, the right woman,
and then, let's say, it's her problem:
Just don't have children right away.

Well, of course you do,
and who should be babysitting that sticky day
in August when one of *your* kid's kids
nearly chokes to death on a cinnamon jawbreaker?
Well, of course, who else could it be? It's you!

At the Regional Hospital

Let's say you've just been caught
admiring the scenery on Highway 12
so fervently you missed that sudden curve
near Kamiah, and there was that infernal
bicyclist along with an almost predictable
spasm of sun you'll later swear
was the only bright moment that afternoon.

Let's say you had just the right amount
of your half-wits about you to swerve
into those new guard rails, the ones that
mar the view of the river but save a life
or two from time to time. This time
let's say it's yours, although your body's
broken here and there, and the car's a wreck.

You're slumped against your seatbelt
thanking whatever gods may be,
lapsing in and out of consciousness,
sunlight, dazzle of river, Selway,
Lochsa, you couldn't say for sure.
Suddenly you remember you were
headed to Missoula, God knows why,
but you rejoice in these random efforts
of the cerebral cortex. And now if only
your ankle would unbend itself from
under the brake pedal and lift you up
from the front seat, it would be nice,
or if your left arm would stop dangling,
or if only that mad confusion of sirens
wailing and whining would stop
and you could hobble away from there,
a little sheepish, your bumper a dim
memory, something metallic clattering
underneath, just your tailpipe, that would be nice.

But no. The EMT says it's broken, says
they've got a good regional hospital here
and they'll take good care of you. His name is Frank
and his voice is gentle. The woman with him,
also wearing a dark blue jumpsuit, her name
is Kathy and she lives in Orofino with her two kids,
one not yet in school, and her ex-husband
lost his job at the mill, thank God, and left town.
Frank says they didn't use to have a regular
full-time doctor, but now, thank the Lord,
they've got two. They agree it's lucky
you had your seatbelt fastened. This, they agree,
thank the good Lord, is your lucky day.

While the grimy mechanic at Clearwater Motors
consigns what's left of your car to the vultures,
the doctors are eager to see what's left of you.
Doctor Stokes, always dreaming of gynecology,
alas, is just a GP but has the best
bedside manner west of the Mississippi.
His partner, Doctor Splintz, was almost
an orthopedic surgeon. That was just before
interning at Cincinnati General where,
he says, the bones never set just right
because of the humidity. Out here in Idaho,
he says, bones behave differently.

You'll be okay, they agree. No need to operate.
No need to call the helicopter to chop you up
to Spokane and that costly crew of specialists.
They can do it all here. They can set an elbow
as well as the next fellow, they assure you.
Your insurance is good. By the time you're up
and around, your car will be as good as new,
maybe. There's always a certain amount of risk.

Halibut: See Flatfish

All fish are funny, incapable of escaping
their profound finniness or their silly
often silvery bilateral symmetry,
but these halibut and their flatfish
cousins—flounder, turbot, sole—
have found a way to be even funnier.
One eye migrates to the other side
of the tiny head, left or right
depending on the species.
While all fish are funny in the way
they school and flicker, display themselves
in air, perhaps inflate from fear,
flip foolishly at our feet
when out of their element,
the goofy halibut and their relatives
turn themselves half inside out,
lie white side down against the sandy floor
and blend (see "pigmentation").
Largest of the lot the halibut
feed voraciously on other fish with their
capacious mouth and sharp, strong teeth.
They prefer cold water
perhaps four hundred fathoms deep
where oxygen is no joke
whisked through their terrible gills,
perhaps six hundred pounds
and ten or twelve feet long.
None of this humor applies to sharks,
those powerfully dumb devouring machines.
No, this only applies to the harebrained halibut
gone paunchy in their middle age
and a bit too scarce of late
the fishermen say.

We'll be reduced to perch if this keeps up,
witless, devoid of punch-lines.
The fishermen lower their deepest running nets
searching for those lay-down comedians,
those funny, funny guys.
They know we all need a good laugh.

Feeling Strongly Both Ways

In this class the engineers,
civil, electrical, mechanical, chemical,
do not understand ambivalence.
They cannot conceive of
conceiving of things
both ways at once.
It seems wrong to them.
And the more the poets in class
agree to be ambivalent,
the more the engineers talk
about dropping the course.

The engineers transfer to physics,
Elementary Quantum Mechanics,
where free particles
sprinkle the mental landscape,
hydrogen atoms
come untethered,
and perturbation theory
quavers through a universe of quarks.
Ecstatic without poetry
the engineers agree
about the esthetics of ambiguity.

To Be Poor

is to inherit poverty, no will
necessary,
        but the scenery,
the scenery shapes up around them
beautifully,
        tamaracks turning gold
as the old Indian-head coins
sold on television
after the late show,
        quaking aspen
trembling in the icy wind.
They bequeath all they have,
all their rage
        and bitterness,
an old Ford wearing cinderblocks
for tires
        and bleeding rust
and looking out at the costly world
through cracked and splintered
windshields.
        For trustees they say,
"What the hell, who can we trust?"

The Man Who Kept Waking Up

One day he began waking up
early, unknown birds
calling from the gray dawn
like boyhood friends
whistling him up for a baseball game.

He woke up solemnly, his mind
making slow thoughts—coffee,
ballglove, mow the lawn, warblers,
go to the office. His wife
slept beside him deeply as if
nothing bad had happened as usual
in the past twenty years.

She had almost forgotten she
was the farmer's daughter
yawning at first light
and he was the yankee salesman,
and their life had turned
into a kind of bad boy's joke
gone west and north beyond mocking-
birds. Must be just robins,
she thought as she fell back to sleep.

But he kept on waking up and up,
nagging himself with half-dreams
like stories with missing parts,
beginning here, middle there,
ending nowhere.
In one dream their daughter
shaved her head like a punk rocker
and said the cops had busted her
for possession. In another his wife
confided he was a terrible lover
and his hair fell out all over.

Every morning for the rest of his life
the man kept waking up early,
but he could not leave his bed until
he could hear his wife and daughter
arguing in the kitchen, or his wife
alone making noisy black coffee,
and the unknown birds growing silent.

The Inner Ear

It was May and more than they could resist,
the first red flush of Indian paintbrush,
blue flax, a patch of arnica, and suddenly
a bed of vetch blown in from someone's
wheatfield like a purple quilt, and they were
off their bikes and sprawling in the sun.

That night she lay on her pillow and listened
to the swish of passing cars, the distant
drawl and growl of a swag-bellied semi
hauling wood chips down to the mill,
but this was not the music she desired.

She thought if she listened the right way,
if she lifted her head away from the dream
she could feel pursuing her, she could hear
what the stream had been trying to say
that afternoon, or the wind, or the slurred
song of the vireo in the apple tree gone wild.

But what she heard directly entered her ear
and tickled first, then rattled her eardrum
like a snare, and she rose up in frenzy
shrieking. Her lover woke from a half-sleep
leaping with rainbow trout, sun-drowsed.
Their first clear thought was a wood tick.

And long before they reached the hospital
she could feel the heat, the fever,
nausea, pain that would rack her body,
could see the pink spots she had seen before
on a girl at summer camp. Then suddenly,
as if imagination exhausted itself, nothing.
A stillness and a deep and inner quiet.

When they flushed her ear, out came a tiny
butterfly, pale yellow, dead, she guessed,
from trying to listen too intently.
She could not resist the whimsy, wondering
what it was this Northwest Ringlet,
as her lover called it, heard in those last
dark flutterings before it died.

One Version of the Facts

Chapter One keeps happening over and over.
Women come home from work in the city
dressed fit to kill, fetch their kids
from day care, grab the largest butcher knife
in the kitchen and start chopping up
the chicken.
          That's all, just cutting chicken.
The kids start babbling. She slaps them
in front of the television, ritual cartoon
violence, the usual mayhem, predictable justice.
Power Rangers. If they want candy, she gives it,
gives it.
          Home come the hungry husbands, late,
frustrated, overgrown babies, powerdrunk,
underappreciated. The wives are absolutely not
having the right thing for dinner, no matter
what it is.
          She thinks how happy she was
leaving the office when a cool afternoon breeze
whipped under her slip and teased her skirt,
and her heels clicked smartly down the sidewalk.

Woman with Roses

After collecting the blossoms of her lovers,
she stores them up as potpourri in bowls,
mostly dry rose petals almost
black with longing.

Sometimes she waits until they're dry,
then pulverizes them
and stitches them in small
embroidered bags she makes herself.

These she scatters as sachets
among her bras and panties,
intimate with her slips and negligees,
so after all these years

her lovers linger still,
and she can see them, touch them,
smell them, not as they were,
but as they should have been.

In the long silence
that defines her life as she creates it
day by day, occasionally
broken by Brahms or Debussy,

love comes and goes.
Months pass, a man bearing roses
shows up out of nowhere,
where the others came from,

and she shows him
more than he wants to know,
shows him so much
she cannot do anything except

what she does best,
which is to disappear
like pollen riding on the wind
without so much as a sigh.

Maintenance

Behind the check-out desk,
nestled under the counter
cover to cover with
Lady Chatterley's Lover
and *Tropic of Cancer*,
lurk the most popular
volumes, nearly as valuable
as rare incunabula:
the Chilton repair manuals
dating all the way back,
and although you cannot
check them out, they are black
from the passionate grease
of burned-out bearings,
blurred with sweat that falls
from the brows of men
desperate to save money
by installing junkyard
slave cylinders, rebuilt
carburetors, power brake
boosters. How painstakingly
they read each hard word,
index fingers inching along the
sentences, smudge by smudge,
their lips puckered
by the challenges of language,
diagrams that make
perfectly good sense, but
words that disintegrate
at the touch, words that
crack under the strain
like worn seals, timing belts,
fuel pumps, hoses, valves,
like love, so much
that can go wrong.

To a Nunnery Go

When Saint Catherine's threatened to go belly up
as the wheat farmers lost their faith in Pakistan
buying at four-and-a-quarter a bushel,
and the roof threatened to cave in and the floor
to buckle under the weight of rampant sin,
and the farmer's only daughter got pregnant
again instead of taking the veil, Father Schroeder
got married and opened a bed-and-breakfast
there in the old convent next to the best cathedral
Bavarians could buy in nineteen-ten, red brick
and stained glass windows, stations of the cross
gilded with ore from the Coeur d'Alenes up north.

The new priest, young and empty of ambition,
unattractive, unathletic, unintelligent,
but full of vague desire, broods in the confessional.
The farmers' daughters yawn from sin to sin,
their mothers aren't much better, and their sons
spend Sundays watching television. City-slickers
pay whatever it takes to make love in the old convent
where a young novitiate once bled to death,
the cleaning woman says, from ecstasy.

In the priest's worn copy of the *Little Pictorial Lives*,
Saint Catherine of Alexandria is stripped and scourged,
tortured, raped, and murdered by some soldiers,
her body wafted away by angels from the grave
to heaven, of course, a lesson in "perseverance and
fidelity to grace." But on this quiet summer night
violence and history are out of place
as the young priest, strolling past the convent,
hears a woman's voice, excited, crying "yes."

Spring Day in Spokane, 1993

At the Finch Arboretum that barely spring afternoon
children not yet fully blended by the schools
played on the grass, still fresh in its first cutting,
and the grinning reaper puttered up the hill
riding his blood-red mower. Birds sang a-cappella,
shrill tunes piercing the steel growl and mutter
of freeway traffic. Sporting fresh green paint
the park benches gleamed in the fragile sun.
A river copper beech limbered up for the season
beside a well-aimed stream a child could jump across.
We met at a bronze plaque: "Japanese Barberry."

Three blocks north a woman with blue-gray hair
lay tight and motionless in green polyester slacks
against the curb, her old myopic eyes
disturbing no one, her glasses fractured.
We watched a nervous crowd flutter around her,
anonymous urban flattery, passive as pigeons
feeding at random. The angry driver behind us
lay on his horn for dear life, so we turned off
at the next block for lunch. We talked about
life in Idaho, the menu, the chubby marmots
scrambling on the rocks below. You said
they were exterminating these rodents
down in Lewiston where they burrow
into the levee. Professional killers, marmot
hit-men using poison, traps, and guns.

Two thousand miles southeast another mad savior
transubstantiated ordinary pine with liquid fire
into smoke and ashes, the charred remains
of a couple dozen sad children, a few score

deranged adults, heat so intense the prairie dogs
withered, and bob white quail by whip-poor-will
the birds grew silent. We watched the river,
swollen with snow-melt, plunge
over the dark basalt to generate power,
a simple and cold, fast eloquence broken,
you recalled, by the random plummet of a transient,
nameless and depressed in February, one more
alcoholic mother mistaking the falls for a mirror.

The Kinesthetics of Aging

Suddenly, at fifty-three to be so deeply
concerned about the left knee,
not the right, which seems to be
holding up well enough considering,
means to be thinking twice before
bending to the floor in search of
anything worth less than a quarter,
and taking it under advisement
whether genuflection
signifies that much to God by now.

To be nurturing second thoughts about
the wisdom of playing soccer
one last season after forty, having lost
confessedly a step or three
against a rare phenomenon of nature:
youth that youngers up itself
with every game and scrimmage,
means to be finding oneself
curious about the gross anatomy of knees,
the mystic language of the joints:

patella, meniscus, anterior cruciate,
all cartilage and ligaments,
the brotherhood of cheerful arthro-
scopic patients, some having witnessed
their own grim cutting, and then
the rehabilitations, the exotic posturings
of knee braces, the new breakthroughs
haunting one's knee-elevated sleep.

To be knee-bent toward oblivion,
knee-deep in September
means one has come from somewhere
beyond Alabama, ready to hobble
the rest of the way smiling
through the tight, circling pain.
There's a stumbling beauty to it all.

Early Retirement

A few years down the road I see myself
sounding my barbaric yawp from the rooftop
of the new addition to the university library.
Below, stumbling heedless to their next class,
most of my former students ignore me
as custom dictates, but a precious few
look up as if distracted by one of Rilke's
awful angels. "Yawp!" I am yelling, "Yawp!"
At the top of my exhausted lungs, "Yawp!"

"Isn't that the guy I had for world lit last fall?"
the tall blonde asks herself nervously,
wondering if I might change her grade
when I get down, a B she knows she didn't
quite deserve, an aberration, she now sees,
of a disturbed mind. She feels terribly sorry
for herself. She thought about dropping the course,
but I convinced her to stay for Ibsen's sake
and she was grateful and never forgave Nora
for walking out on her husband and kids,
or Emma Bovary for playing around.

Deciding I will neither jump nor change her grade,
she turns away, and the next to come along
is a happy scholar-athlete who recognizes me
by name as the source of his most recent D.
"That's McFarland," he calls out. "He's weird!"
"Hey Bryan," I cry, "yawp!" I personalize it.
I'm one of those profs who get to know his students
just well enough to write a good blackmail note:
(quote) "I got evidence how you really spell.
Send me ten thousand bucks each year
the rest of your career in the NFL." (unquote)

Clouds begin to scud, and scudding clouds
worry me. The wind grows chill. The lowing herd
of humanity picks up pace with the jingling bell.
By all rights I should be out to pasture now,
or at least in the classroom wheedling for my supper.
"Please, what *is* Romanticism? Name any three
famous Romantic poets," I yawp piteously.

Being Seen

When will you see me next?
Always less predictable than weather,
I can show up anytime
anywhere you least expect me.
Don't bother to prepare.
Just keep plenty of everything on hand,
beer in the fridge, some bourbon,
peanut butter, cheese and crackers,
maybe some large green olives
with pits still in them
where they damned well belong
until we're ready to spit them out
across your fence into the pasture.

Be ready to talk all night with me
about nothing consequential,
least of all our intimate selves.
No one overhearing us will know.
They will suppose we are just
good friends who broke a word or two
together on occasion,
fractured a sudden impulse
into strange music. That's okay.

You say the bears have learned
how to undo the hasp locks on the barn,
claw their way into your birdseed,
and sip the red, sugary nectar
from your feeders,
cuffing the hummingbirds aside.
Like those bears I'm a thief at heart,
so be on the lookout for me after dark.
Like those bears I can take
anything not nailed down
whenever you least expect.

II. Certain Women (1977)

Certain Women

Women like that cannot stand tenderness.
Not of their flesh,
                your soft caress
wears like a cold stare.
Velvet over larynx, skin over granite
their voices quarry hard words,
             worry in garnet,
             grief in jade,
no remorse. Your sympathy
grates on the air.
Women like that prefer brief farewells.
Not to their taste,
                your lingering
where dew licks the leaf.

The Lentil Queen

Heir apparent to the peas,
you ease the hard red wheat
beneath the combine
green as a crown jewel,
jasmine cigarettes censing the cab.

What does your wheat whisper
under a cold half moon?
"Remember Ceres beautiful as you.
We feel her presence in our roots,
feel her pain in your sickle. Beware."

Smiling through this myth
you choose to reap the lentils,
glean a circle in the yellow rape.
Farmers across the ridge
scratch their heads, what does it mean?

You bend the brim of your leather hat.
"I have my beauty. I fear nothing.
Tomorrow I disk the wheat stubble
quietly, relentless. What does it mean?
I flourish. I am the lentil queen."

Child's Backyard in Winter

Beneath the leafless apple tree the sand
congeals in its wooden frame
freezing her casual pail-shaped castle,
the destined summer residence
for the czar of all the Russias.

Her swing hangs rigid,
link soldered to link, a crystal statue
formed of steel and solid water
that soared to supple mach twelve
thirty days ago.

Her jump rope slung over the clothesline
is like summer hung out to dry,
caught in winter,
now braided in ice
with cold red handles clacking in the wind.

Tenth Anniversary

Even at two the moon shines high and bright,
his mind anticipating pancakes
and tomorrow's mail. And her body
lies in a heap of soft breath
wearing its most impregnable gown
woven of faded daffodils on blue
reproach.
        Yet before she rolled over, two
thousand miles in the same bed,
she said the moon was silver
and her love was glowing in the dark
like a jaguar's eyes,
           and when he asked
where, she said she was tired
and buried herself in blankets,
and when he reached for her
she swatted him with palm fronds.

At the Nursing Home

Here is an old wife awaiting death.
She has refined her life
to one story
        with gestures.
How she canned vegetables one fall
enough to last all winter
        in central Idaho
when her sister was there.
She tells it again
as her fingers stir the air
        peeling apples,
        slicing carrots,
        snapping beans.
Again that legend. John, her husband,
        loved his applesauce.
Only one jar failed to seal.

III. Composting at Forty (1984)

Have Fun?

for Richard Hugo

We are getting drunk. The music
is like the war, your bombs
vaguely scattering among docile cows.
You keep asking for "Tuxedo Junction"
and each time it plays you laugh,
maybe remembering that blockbuster
that blew up the swastika factory.
That was Dorsey, that was Miller, this is whiskey.

We aren't having fun. These women,
they are all gray and they keep on
getting grayer whenever you touch them.
The waitresses, especially the young blondes,
turn grayest of all, and quickest.
Good friends' wives are always gray,
and grayest just before they fade away.

Tomorrow we'll fish the Clearwater,
and the water will be gray. We'll drink
coffee, rub our heads, swear off
these funny drunks. We'll talk
about anything but women, Italy,
Glenn Miller, food, and poetry.
You will drive to Montana alone,
tell everyone there that you had fun.

The Hanford Wives

East of us the vineyards grow
in orderly rows,
trellised for full exposure
to our quick summers.
Here in Richland, Kennewick, Pasco,
suburbs of a city that does not exist,
we study our lives
in brief verses,
we, the Hanford wives.

In summer the amaranth and artemisia
slip into our yards
leaving their common names
(tumbleweed, sagebrush) like the names
of old lovers
irrevocably seeded.
We pretend not to notice,
tell our husbands to mow the lawn
quick, before something gets hold.

Dust can storm in here
from any direction, blotting the sun.
North of us something
more unstable than ourselves
happens in a language
even the sun would not understand.
Bees keep my husband occupied
when he's not with the reactor.
The children love it.

Hide-and-Seek

Kimberley always counts too fast, afraid
when she turns around and opens her
half-shut eyes she will not even see
a small foot twitch the lower branch
of the lilac bush, or sense the nervous
grip of Jennifer's fingers on the old
half-rotted pie apple tree, or even
hear the subtle gasps of breath withdrawn
from the air. And everything will darken.

When she hides she steers clear of that place
under the wheelbarrow in a black corner
of the garage where small gray spiders
annihilate flies and hold dried bees
fading in dusty webs, or that place
near the dense forsythia where she might
slither in a coil so tight and so obscure
her sister might not find her, or might
send her one-two-three, shrill and sudden,
shivering across her bare shoulders.

When she seeks she looks for open space
as if her friends would wrap themselves
in sun or sprawl like spokes
among the dandelions. If they are hidden well
it might be better not to find them,
let them smile or tremble in whatever shade
they have secured. Kimberley doesn't like
surprises, doesn't like the silence of still
breathless forms, her sister hanging from a tree
like moss, friends like lizards lurking
in stone shadows, all their dread
drawn up around them like scaly skin.

For her the joy of this game only comes
with shrieks of *home-free*, swift
transitions into tag, shift
of quiet smiles to laughter, lift
of voices into lively leap-frog,
hop-scotch, jump-rope twirling light.

Asotin Girl Still Lost

When the Ferris wheel pins itself to the moon
a twelve-year-old girl might pass
for a woman.
                    Pedaling her bike along
Snake River, Christine might see the moon
trickling downstream, feel
                              that sudden response
to the moon
and rear up high on the pedals and sing
rare tunes like a Danish merry-go-round.

Then she would peel herself away from
farmboys' animals lowing at the moon
in their ribbon-blue
simplicity, as if a lucky cast of glossy eyes
or human-sounding notes
                              might save their throats.
Christine, you rode The Hammer
                              throwing your glad
screams into the night of men and moons.
You were young and old at once.

What happened later, when the gears of The Whip
stiffened?
                    I think, Christine, you heard the moon
ring out eternity,
and your bicycle sliced its choppy trail,
                              its river-silky light,
                              its doubtful path,
like a hand over a mouth.

Town Librarian

Ethel Magruder's false teeth click
through chicken salad sandwiches thick
with mayonnaise. "Be still,"
she whispers from behind her winesap.
Her eyes blaze, if only they could kill.
Her own waxed paper rattles in her lap.

To the right of her brown bag,
adult fiction hovers like a hag
over a cauldron. Across the hall
adult non-fiction rests
unmolested, Gibbon's *Decline and Fall*,
Grant's *Memoirs*, Dewey's *Quest*.

When her small eyes blink
on the apple, children slink
into Commager's *Blue and Gray*
with the Brady photographs,
scattering to their proper place
when the waxed paper stirs.

Checking out *The Sea for Sam*, you wonder
about those violent forbidden men at Sumter,
those yawning eyes at Malvern Hill,
that icy drummer boy buried at Shiloh,
Ethel Magruder, alone with Henry Miller,
alone with the icy drummer boy.

October Soiree

I nightmare a gray orgy,
bland shirts striped a muted blue
and cheese-poked mouths
strumming The Department
like an old guitar.

On the cutting-board my hand
tightens into a roll of salami
hard and garlic strong
against the talk and talk
about the talk. Suddenly
they all get subjunctive,

could, and should, and if
I were
I would.
Then the women cross their legs
in unison, intransitive,
feet dangling.

The beer turns indefinite.
The wine runs free
as an idle memory.
I remember when every fool
I made of myself was funny.

"Bring on the hard stuff," I say,
somebody's face going gray
as my dreams of fame.
Someone's sinuous fingers
float to the sour cream.
Behind me the music
hums like a bloated locust,
remnant of summer
gone fat on the fondue.

Spinning, I grab the nearest breast.
"Any port in a storm!" I shout
above her shriek. Feet shuffle,
lights go out. The last voice
is the chairman crooning an old tune,
"If you believed in me."

There's Something Suspicious

All my life I've been followed.
Black Buicks with dark-haired
vaguely foreign men
flex the highway behind me.
At night their headlights
probe my spine like fingers
tightening a sponge.

In winter footprints trace the snow
around my house.
My neighbor says it's just the dogs,
some mastiff breed with nondescript paws.
My neighbor
speaks with a strange accent.
Blue-eyed, he's the right age
for an old Gestapo agent.
Lately he's taken to wearing black
calf-length leather coats.

When I'm gone they'll find
my drawers stuffed with odd
keys. These will fit
uncertain doors, deposit boxes,
lockers in bus terminals
in small towns, ignitions of red
Alfa-Romeos, sky-blue Maseratis.

When I'm gone they'll find
my drawers crammed with
unfinished poems, subtle evocations,
passionate shudders, profane breaths:
"The rat crawled up her . . ."
sordid spaces. See?
Those aliens in big cars,
those leathered men who plod
about my house on snowy nights, they'll see,
they'll see there's more to all this
than meets the eye.

Composting at Forty

You thought, just after dawn
to belly up in your great green
gorging truck, as you have always done,
and cram the rinds of my oranges,
succulent honeydew, exotic coffee grounds
into your iron maw.
No more. Now I'm plowing it all back in,
reinvesting it along with grass clippings, cigars
and other bad old habits
in this bank of dirt.
I am cultivating a new reverence
for the undevoured, for all the small
unsavory things of the earth,
for all the half-cooked peas,
burnt beans, stale crusts of bread, eggshells.
By God
they shall be nobly put to use
through intercession of the acids,
friction, heat, the weight of soil,
rain and melting snow dissolving
their weak identities
for a new, rich, dark and fertile earth.

Fonk's Goes Under

When the last dime store went under
prices dived for days. Shoppers
strange to the manager seeped
in, then poured until
he propped the doors open,
fore and aft, and still they streamed
in from the parking lot,
in from the street,
in from the shopping centers outside town.

At first the counters held,
Duvella's luncheonette to port,
men's sportshirts starboard,
hardware, toys and tropical fish
for ballast.
But then the galley cooled.
Duvella told the reporter
about those couples and the war,
the mirror with Guadalcanal dead
reflected when she turned
from certain faces to the grill.

Without Duvella the store listed badly,
took on too much empty
space. Slowly the salesgirls
abandoned their posts
slipping away after five not to return,
replaced by the stern manager,
face hardening to his martyrdom.

At last prices floundered and the store
filled with the smell of dust
and cold popcorn.
Plastic fire trucks with missing wheels,
tin boats without motors,
unmatched socks and empty hangers,
these were the flotsam on a slick
of memories and outdated profits.

At Main Street's edge
old-timers gather reminiscing of oiled floors,
propeller fans, Duvella,
the old man whose son tried hard
but didn't have it, the new manager,
what was his name?
Went down with the last dime store.

"A Multitude of Birds"

—St. Francis of Assisi

Sing now the desperate dance of small birds.
Sing where the quail collect after snowfall,
the mud-guttered borders of roads where the last
hard grains of wheat lay heaped with the gravel.

Sing the wren's last colorless song,
the solitary vireo's slow cold slur
by the roadside sifting old brown bags
for crusts or bread crumbs, or perhaps

among the shards of bright green glass
a sip of wine, a claret deep as blood.
Sing then the cunning of sparrows which look
like nothing but dark little rocks,

for they will endure, and the starling
whose song is the echo of anything,
and the waxwing, gregarious feeders.
Sing warblers and blackbirds perched on the edge

of winter with ice clinging fast
to their wings, with plentiful seed
lying deep, with songs frozen hard into words.
Sing now the dance of the small birds.

Palouse History

The history of wheatfields
is not easily written.
Mostly it's wind
and the movements of dust,
shifting of snow.
From below the surface
rocks and stones
keep edging up
as if they had
something to mutter to the sun.
Local history
comes and goes
in the stubble.
Like men and women
each crop thinks
it has something new to tell.
Here and there a shotgun shell,
a tuft of feathers
offer their temporary testimony.
One of the stones
may be an arrowhead.
On the rocky cilia
broken trucks and plows,
weathered combines
rust peacefully.
Board by board, roofs first,
old barns and houses collapse.
The wheatfields
write a quiet book,
only the cries of hawks and mice
for punctuation.

No Demand

Twenty years ago there was maybe sixty gypos
between Clarkia and Helmer, Bovill,
over around Potlatch. Maybe a hundred.
Six or a dozen trucks apiece, couple loaders,
get yourself a crew,
couple fellers'll cut first,
drink later,
you could do business.
Hell, nobody ever got rich at it,
only the mills, but it beats a desk.
By God dangerous, too.
Keep your wits about you,
keep your head screwed on.
You'd be surprised how easy . . .
just a glance at a ground squirrel
at the wrong time,
widow-makers, broke chains,
some damn green kid riding a Cat
don't know shit from Shinola
buries your best friend
before you can blink the sweat from your eyes.
And suddenly you remember
you heard his last word,
"Hey!"
Colder'n a witch's teat, or hot,
raw dust sucking your lungs,
and the women get tired of it,
tired of you, tired of your snoose.
My old lady up and flushed a whole can of Copenhagen
down the toilet, brand new.
That done it.
So you don't get nowhere,
and if you've got kids
they don't amount to nothing,
teacher says they oughta go to college.
Then's when you get laid off,

wonder where the money went.
Boss says he's sorry, says
you always busted your gut,
says you'll be the first called back,
says it to the next five guys as well.
Now there couldn't be no more than twenty
and some of them down pretty low,
gypos, what the hell. No demand.
Got arthritis in both hands
so bad I couldn't set a choker,
back's no good.
I'd go back in a minute if I could.

Bad Lunch at Cottonwood, Idaho

Where wheat laps gently at the city limits
avoid seafood, even tuna salad,
and smiling waitresses
graduated from high school directly
into nylon dresses with large pockets
jangling at the waist.
           In Seattle
there was only the soft rustle of currency
on taffeta, and the sound of seawater rushing
through barnacles, and the waitress was old,
efficient and hopeless.
                Ironmonger to all
southeast Ohio, my father taught me
to trust Businessman's Specials
when the chips are down, in restaurants
where orange plastic splits in booths
and the varnish glues your napkin
to somebody's phone number. Beware
of sticky saltshakers. Beware
of waitresses with crooked teeth. Beware
of hamburgers with a nom-de-pume.
                Cottonwood is no place
for Salisbury Steak of dubious gravy
or Salmon Croquettes torn from the sea's dark womb.

Idaho Requiem

for Robert Lowell

Out here, we don't talk about culture,
we think we are. We nurtured Ezra Pound
who ran from us like hell
and never came back. You
never came at all. You
will never know how clever
we never are out here.
You never drank red beer.
You never popped a grouse
under a blue spruce just because it was there.

Tell us about Schopenhauer and your friends
and fine old family. We left ours
at the Mississippi, have no names left
to drop. We spend our time
avoiding Californians and waiting
for the sage to bloom, and when it does
we miss the damn things half the time.
When a stranger comes in we smile
and say, "Tell us about yourself."
Then we listen real close.

But you would say, "I've said what I have to say."
Too subtle, perhaps, for a can of beer,
too Augustan for the Snake River breaks.
But how do you know this wasn't just
the place to die? Why not have those
kinfolk ship your bones out here, just
for irony's sake? We keep things plain
and clear because of the mountains.
Our mythology comes down to a logger
stirring his coffee with his thumb.

IV. *The Haunting Familiarity of Things (1993)*

Out Here

Even a stone can astonish us,
thrown or underfoot, rippling the surface
of some dark pond
or stumbling along in the dust
if we give it a chance.

In New York, L.A., Chicago, even Seattle
passions run riot in ways we cannot
feel with our stingy sensibilities.
People keep on living there as if
they were going to die
in the next minute,
so of course they do.
A friend who works for the *Wall Street Journal*
says it's the only honest way to live.

Out here we live as if
we're going to live forever.
We spend carefully.
The Forest Service and the B.L.M.
send college students into the field
each summer to count sagebrush.
They are contemplating a program
to tabulate tumbleweed,
full employment year-round.
It's an education.

The friend from Manhattan
visits one of our short summers,
waiting daily for something to happen.
It never does. The whole summer
is like skipping stones
late in the afternoon on a placid pond.
We try to talk, but she's too deep,
like a stone seeking the bottom.
Out here we like those conversations
where no one has the last word.

Ceteris Paribus

(Other Things Being Equal)

Up and down she would hop
squeaking "hic, haec, hoc"
as if to cheer us into declension.

We will never forget her patrician
disregard for the garter snake
coiled quite dead
in her top drawer,
or the Senecan grace
with which she endured
parental complaints over grades
she made up in the suppressed
orgy of her spinster's head
and delivered with gladiatorial dread.

Danny Ennis, she would say,
her small white hand
saluting her tight-buttoned neck,
conjugate "weep" or "sigh,"
decline "love" or "pleasure."
But no one could do it
the way she could.

Some days, locked between Caesar and Ovid,
when Sherry Harris wore her
cheerleading skirt and sweater
and Wayne McLeroy wore his
football jersey, number forty-four,
she could translate
everything we were thinking
or were ever going to think.

Little Jack

When Little Jack said I'd better come along
with him and his slick black hair,
thick sideburns and leather jacket, I knew
he wouldn't take no for an answer,
so I drove him out to the lake
in my '49 Olds with its two-piece
front windshield, plush seats, hydromatic
(whatever that was) and that fine blue
plastic cap on the steering wheel
featuring Saturn among the stars.

We stopped in the dark and Little Jack,
not admiring the constellations, scrambled
fearless of snakes, through thick
tangles of palmetto to where he'd stashed the beer,
stolen of course, no one needed to tell me that.
He slipped a case into the trunk while I
searched the rearview mirror nervously for cops
looming in the shadows, leaning tight,
guns drawn, beneath the moonlit pines.
As usual, I saw nothing.

We drove the rutted road to the lakefront,
Little Jack limiting his conversation to a belch,
Little Jack not being much for small talk,
Little Jack preferring to let his switchblade
talk for him most of the time.
Perhaps he stuttered, grew tongue-tied,
amazed at the dazzling jabber of those of us
who carried solid C averages, even in Latin.
Perhaps cheerleaders and majorettes left him,
as they did most of us, utterly speechless.
Perhaps his father, before he drifted away
on a sea of whiskey, beat all the right words
out of him. He never could say the right thing.

We had hardly lifted our sky-blue cans,
silently toasting our badness, before a squad car
hit us with its lights and a voice from the dark
accused us of being.
                            A slick lie leaped to my lips,
but my tongue thickened on it and my throat
constricted. Before I knew it I collapsed
in a heap of black, self-serving honesty
as Little Jack sat in the back of the squad car
alone and sullen on the cold leather seat.

Thereafter, as the desk sergeant warned,
I followed the straight and narrow,
keeping myself aimed toward Saturn and the high
difficult stars, the ways of right and wrong
as neatly divided as my front windshield.
Accessory after the fact, I was released
to the custody of my incredulous father, whose life
knew no iniquity. All he could ask was why.
And I, who had nearly all the answers then,
being sixteen, had nothing to say.

Burning the Bad Nuns

This afternoon I burned the four Peruvian nuns
you may have heard about a few months ago,
the ones caught smuggling drugs in their
old habits, having been expelled from the order.

Dry raspberry canes gave flare to my fire,
but mostly I burned them the old Spanish way,
in the slow green sizzle of apple branches
pruned from the trees to improve the fruit.

Puffing my two-dollar cigar, I gave
hardly a second thought to their Third World
souls gone up in smoke or to their once proud
families in disgrace, brothers living in squalor,
their fathers dead from cholera.

Feeling religious for the first time in years,
I righteously raked their gray ashes,
believing they would nurture my garden.
Then I sprayed them till they turned black.

Cooling down, I recalled how then my face
burned, how my resilient rage rekindled
in their shame and how the merciless sweat
streaked my glasses and poured down my cheeks
like tears in tropical camouflage.

Lord, what heat those gloomy ladies gave!
Later I found my eyebrows singed from
moving too close, wanting to save no stick,
no, not one clipping from that conflagration.

Orgy

Clicking and scraping, the buttons and zippers
awaken me from my drunken half-sleep.
Inside the dryer the clothes are throwing a party,
an orgy of sleeves and half-slips, bras,
tossed about like straws in a gale of lust,
jockey shorts clinging ecstatically to silken
bikini panties, my gray polyester dress slacks
clinging wantonly to some woman's silver negligee.

My God, it's my wife! But what's a woman like her
doing in a place like this? The lewd heat, the cheap
perfume, the tawdry darkness in the corners,
the monotonous rock and roll of a local group,
idle chatter, a storm of romantic boredom.
You call this an atmosphere for love?

Awake, my dove! Come out in your warm
wetness and cavort with me under the stars.
Let us reach overhead and pluck the strings
of the sky's violin. Let us dance all night
in the cool wind and waken at dawn refreshed,
side by side in the calm, dry certainty of ourselves.

Fourth of July in Buhl, Idaho

We missed the Sagebrush Days parade,
and the town closed down around us
with a vengeance, sidewalks
rolling up like old window blinds.

Wind spits cottonwood branches at us now,
trying to sleep in a friend's back yard
amid firecrackers, our tattered spirits
lifting over the Snake River plain.

We plan to breakfast at the old Ramona
where Clark Gable once said frankly
he didn't give a damn, then off to see
the World Famous Balanced Rock.

Maybe the Green Giant holds this town
in the palm of his jolly hand,
and he will gather us godlike into his
rich and indivisible love.

They say this town is all edges
bound up in bouquets of sagebrush,
a dry joke of a gift, free to blow away.
I know a guy who fell in love here twice.

Home from Vacation

Nothing seems quite right.
The neighbors wave as if we were strangers
or worse,
   long lost relatives.
        The lawn,
watered and cut at unfamiliar angles
by the boy down the block,
doesn't look right.
      The quiet relief of our
own front door feels odd.

Miles slip from our stiff shoulders,
the burden of that restored fort
near the Wyoming border,
        Disney's gut-
wrenching roller coasters,
       that motel in Iowa
where the air conditioner moaned
helplessly all night.

We bewilder ourselves.
Who left these coffee grounds to mold all month?
Who forgot to throw away
      this half-loaf of
hard, gray-green, furry bread?
       Is this really
our last chance to renew *Time*? Can time be
renewed?
     Who *were* these people who
left these grotesque artifacts?

Now we must make things right by forgetting
the drought-red sun
                              setting over a hill in
Belmont County, Ohio,
                              visits to the graves
of misremembered relatives who spelled the
family name incorrectly for some
unfathomable reason.

Time now to call and have the newspaper
aim us back into time and place.
                              Time to
open the windows, brew a pot of coffee,
to make things right,
to sink into that dark leather chair that looks
                              hauntingly familiar.

Spring Comes to the Clearwater

Outside Kooskia, Idaho
where the mill closed last week,
April stirs in the roots of grass
as if everyone had work.

Daffodils don't give a damn
that the hardware store
closed forever last month
or that some hard-luck logger
shot the guy next door.

The river blunders along
leaving boulders to bleach in the sun
like the vertebrae of
long dead animals
thrown by the roadside.

Casual brown butterflies
quietly fling themselves
at windshields.

About those boys who
liquored themselves into a fatal
bend of the river yesterday
the crocus, white and yellow,
have nothing to say.

Skywalking

The first year he imagined fear away,
fell to an empty pretense
propped with noise and beer at the
nearest earth-hugging bar.
He suspected the Mohawks wore
eagle feathers under their silver
hard hats, and one day he tried
a nervous joke, a pigeon feather,
but it didn't work. Each night,
he would throw up his false courage
and flush it into the Hudson.

The second year he found a girlfriend.
Love held him tight to the girders.
He learned how to be afraid
gracefully, and after a jittery
day's work he would walk home
blessing the firm earth.
He practiced looking up and dreaming into
clouds, usually shaped like women.
At night he held the woman close
and buried his face in her straw-colored hair.

The third year he found himself at home
in the air. He learned to stride steel
on the balls of his feet, to think of it
as turf and of sky as nothing more than
breathing room. Some days he would
shrug the clouds from his shoulders
and dream of nothing at all.
Now he needed neither bars
nor women with straw-colored hair.
Years would pass before he would fall
fearless and without making believe
into the pitiless air.

Town Marshal

Small towns like this, mills belly-up
about like me, don't need but one cop.
Main thing is to know
everyone's business like your own.
I grew up in this town,
busted my back at the mill,
took over marshal when no one else
wanted it. I got divorced so fast
I almost didn't get married first.

Don't need no damn diploma
for this sorta work,
just common sense and knowing
when to grin, when to cut the bull.
Get along with the high school kids
you got it made.
I wink at six-packs
on the floor of the back seat,
but no drugs or hard stuff.
Dip a little snuff
with the old boys down at C.J.'s,
find out what's going on,
it's not a hard job.

Now this new council wants a cap and gown,
Police Academy instead of a badge and gun.
Thirty years, and now
some college kid in a coat and tie
tells me I can't run two miles,
I ain't a good cop.
Hell, it's like I told the council,
this town don't need a good cop.

The Little Guys

Me and Jesse started this business
when the bottom fell out of cedar shakes.
All we knew was cedar.
When we was kids back in Washington
we packed shingles and played football,
twenty years and we always had
plenty money in our jeans.
We got married and had kids,
sent them off to college
all on making shakes.
Then comes this recession
and the government always
takes it out on the little guys.

Over on the coast the cedar's
pretty much solid, good for roofs.
Here it's got big rotten hearts
because it's so dry.
Now we're making latticework.
It's a good deal,
use it for fences or dividers
inside or out.
It weathers good.
We were doing good before the slump,
selling lumber to the Japs and all.
Now with the lattices we've got a contract
with this buyer in Portland
where the ex-wife lives with some bum.
We're the little guys—
cedar is all we know.

Boy in Winter

Imagine the sheer pleasure of crushing underfoot
every ice-crusted puddle within a square mile
of your home, and all the freeze
that shrinks adults
                         deep into their sheepskin coats
means nothing to you!
                         In fact you wore your now
unzipped jacket only to humor your mother,
who seems to think cold is death
                           and you might
catch it as you would a football
spiraling into your ice-red hands.
                    Your father
always told you women were odd.
                      You have just lost
your third pair of gloves this winter, so she will
yell when you get home about your hands
falling off,
            and you will be obliged to
wiggle your fingers for her,
                  and if you don't hurry
outside, she will plunge them into scalding water
and ask if that doesn't feel a lot better.
If you're lucky,
           she'll make hot chocolate,
but you can never tell. In the crazy adult
winter that threatens your boyhood, your parents
worry the warmth out of you.
                  Before long
the curiosity of ice is the only thing that makes sense,
that and the thick white fantasy of snow
they say you must now go out and play in
the way they always did.

Connecting Flights

In the darkened car
at the far end of the runway
the farmer's daughter
stares at the night sky
dreaming of San Diego.
Behind her the windbreak pines,
black against the clouds,
tell where her father's wheat
begins or where their house
breaks the horizon.

These turboprops go
nowhere of consequence.
They barely make it in and out
much of the year,
high-class cropdusters,
updrafted junior pilots
jockeying for jet jobs,
working their way up
from the ground.
And she has seen the ground
close up, fingernail and knuckle,
crosswind dust
choking her last thought
short of getting out.

Now Eddie sits beside her
thinking God knows what,
his touch
stiff on her bare shoulder,
thinking dark green
winter wheat
half under the late spring snow
thawing, growing all night,
the next day, all summer,
harvest, the next sowing.

The farmer's daughter stares
hard over the dark hills
to catch the red flicker
of take-off lights, a small
airplane going somewhere,
anywhere at all.

Memories of Elm Street

On Elm Street, cleaned by disease of elm,
the maples patiently wait for their leaves.

The old photographer walks in the promise of shade
awaiting his next heart attack. The branches

reach casually into the February sky like the hands
of tired soldiers who fought on the wrong side.

One of his photographs shows a young German
caught near the Ruhr, a soldier who thought

about dying but decided not. The picture
captured all of this, given the right viewer.

The old photographer watches two leftover leaves
turn on their stems like small brown flags.

The doctor says he should walk, but slowly,
should stroll through the rest of his life, should

shuffle if necessary, taking it easy, easy,
be patient, what have you got to hurry for?

Light etches its way through the branches,
the memories of elm, latent images

saved by the sun's engraving, despite
the gray clouds giving him such thin negatives.

Meeting

Well, the fog will roll in anyway,
folding along soft wheat furrows.

In the dim farmhouse the wife
locks doors, listens to the dog
whining to the air.

The state trooper stops at a café,
sips bad coffee and waits.

Along the obscure highway
walks the inevitable stranger
wearing black for bad luck.

Now it must be the wheat farmer
tired, deep in his whiskey,

driving home from the elevator,
switching his lights against the fog,
who brings them all together.

The Runner

Hundreds stride past the lilac bushes
where his long legs have crumpled
like a crushed paper cup, discarded,
and he tries to clutch his heart two-handed
where it jabs under the flesh and bony ribs
exploding under the heavy aroma, and he thinks,
exhaling the dense fragrance, damn
now he'll have to limp into the back of the pack
and start all over as soon as these
flashing apologetic feet breeze past.

And how embarrassing it is to slip
into this painfully awkward heap
before hardly getting started, and how his wife
will tease about his receding hair. But the pain
striding across his threshold
takes his mind off her foolishness, and the thick
sweet odor of lilac reminds him it's time to rise
right now and join the fun and not
ruin it for everyone before the sun
lowers its warm black curtain.

The Woodcutters

Some poor schnook like you slays himself
each year trying to save himself a few bucks
on firewood, hacking tamarack and white pine
out of the near wilderness in sheer delight
of noise, metallic wracking of the woods
worse than a million magpies, trail bikes,
ravens cracking the air with their squawks.

They draw themselves from warm houses,
love, gardens plump with late tomatoes.
Out in the haunted woods the trees have fallen
all over themselves in criss-cross heaps.
These are rotten, dank with decay.
But the tallest trees may be the deadliest.
A snag suddenly snaps at your chain saw,
clips you in a vicious embrace
without saying a word, just "swish,"
faster than air can carry the sound
to your ear, and before you know it
you are broken everywhere and your blood
creeps into the blackness fresh and unseen.

Or some poor devil yanks the starter cord,
only to turn away at the wrong moment
thinking he heard a bear or cougar
tearing the brush to maul him for dinner.
Then what a surprise your saw has in store
for the flesh and bone of your leg!
Shock alone protects you from the pain
that's killing you while you think you're
crawling back to your pickup, and your mind
cooperates. It sees you at Rusty's Tavern
telling of the mean steel kiss your chain saw
inflicted just above your knee and how,
pouring just one last red beer,
it made you hold your breath forever.

The Old School at Chestnut Level

At Chestnut Level you could go to school
and about the third time you heard Gaul
divided into three parts you might gaze
uphill at the church where your grandfather's grave
lay like a hump of stone-hard lessons in life.
The windows, boarded now, were hard to resist,
letting in more light than Cicero or Socrates
or right angles bisected by sunbeams.

Science classes had no labs except for corn
ripening outside, cows grazing the schoolyard,
wasps nesting in the outhouse. Yet you learned
enough to get you through, and here you are
lining up joists of the skeletal floor, unboarding windows
you looked through on winter afternoons when snow
drifted the roads so full you could almost
coast home on the quick sled of your mind.

Below the stenciled plaster where the ceiling
buckles, a row of blackboards erodes as if erased
in acid the last time something failed to add up.
Now you must track down formulas for lampblack
to paint over the old word problems that keep
coming back for solutions: the young man
waiting at the train station but he has no watch
and the clock stopped at two, and he left home at four,
and the train averages fifty miles an hour.
How does he know whether he has time?

The boys who climbed the bell tower
carved or penciled their names and dated their
endeavors on the narrow door that led to the ladder
you must now repair rung by rung.
They were careful never to look down
until the bell beat the air with its brass
clamor muscling through the playful shrieks of recess,
then down they clambered half wishing never
again to rise above their ordinary height.
No one famous ever went to school at Chestnut Level.

Scraping the oak wainscotting that embraces the walls
all around, you wish you were twenty years
younger or maybe you think you should walk slowly away,
leaving the old bricks to crumble like untended tombs.
Down the road and over the hill the old farmhouse
you faintly remember belongs to someone else.
An increasingly distant relative owns the place
you built with your father. He rides a mower
over the ground you used to cut with a two-
handed scythe years ago, when you had time.

A Perfect Day

Man, the blue sky yipes all day
like workshirts on their own time
playing a clumsy game of softball,
and the sun will not go down
without whistling or winking
at a lazy pop fly the outfielder,
who played a little pro ball once,
is too kind to catch, and the wind
cooperates, and the rich grass
bends at the ankles, and the girls,
the women, the grandmothers, bloom
among the dandelions and sweet clover,
all of them wonderfully inarticulate.

God, the meadowlarks pounce on the air
like brief interruptions and carry themselves
away, and the soft hoots of the owl
this morning prophesied their flight
along with the soar of the white ball
and the roar of the shortstop toppling
impossibly after it, and the women's
light laughter and teasing shower of
carelessly gathered grass clippings that stick
to his sweat polished back, and still
the sky delights everyone with its intimations
of something beyond pure color,
and a pair of killdeer suddenly sing out,
surprised by evening.

V. Ballgloves (2000)

First Cleats

Stuffing Kleenex in the toes
of my first kangarooskin cleats
I believed I could almost fly,
but I was hung out to dry
out there in the long orange clay
between first and second base.
I felt I had been betrayed.

This would never have happened
to six-foot-three Uncle Stony
who almost played center field
for the old Washington Senators.
These were his cleats, and his sister,
my mother who never told lies,
told me if I drank five glasses
of homogenized milk a day
I would make the team, grow tall,
and hit three hundred at least.

I drank till I almost bled white,
and when coach gave me the sign
I lurched from the haven of first
head down, feet frantically churning,
fists and heart pumping, my cleats
aimed in a dusty direction
that could have been anywhere.

Ballgloves

The baseball glove you lost that afternoon
in a sun-crazed field gone mad with dandelions
was mine. In my sophomore yearbook you can
find it tucked under my arm just below
my smile of phony confidence.
Does it look like I've made the team?
My best friend, who dreamed of himself
dreaming of baseball, has just been killed
driving his father's big blue Oldsmobile.

We went back to the field and searched
as the sun burned out and my rage
and your tears cooled, and the dandelions
quietly closed in on themselves.
At a garage sale a few weeks later
I found a ballglove with that same
sweat-leather smell and bought it for a song,
not that my old glove could be replaced,
but as a way of erasure. I sat that whole
long season on the bench, my ballglove
growing stiff, the pocket gone hollow.

The next day I bought you a brand new glove
which you have long since lost yourself,
I guess, without a second thought.
My first baseball glove, an old Spalding
my uncle used when he played Class D one season
for the Washington Senators, swallowed my hand,
and no amount of neatsfoot oil could soften its
hard luck. Where did I lose that sweet old
patch of leather? In what bright golden
world of sun-struck dandelions?

Dreaming of Baseball

Late summer nights I dream of baseball
coming back to small towns.
                          Bleachers return
filled with genuine splinters,
so I rent a flat canvas cushion and lean back
arching my spine
               to the next row.

Moths in the lights make better butterflies
than these nine guys
                 make ballplayers.
Behind the stands, preparing for life,
boys shag fouls,
               trade profanities,
invest themselves in casual fistfights.

Three loud women, always the first ones there,
hold court behind home plate.
                   One of them knows me,
even behind my scorecard. I give her my
smallest wave,
           my slenderest smile.

Above the dugout adolescent wives of the home team
languish in blonde boredom.
                 Forcing their squeals,
they hope their husbands will grow up some day
and find real jobs,
            and they can stop
checking groceries, waiting tables.
They all feel pregnant.

I buy a Pepsi from the sad-eyed boy who moves
gloomily through the stands in search of his boyhood.

He drops my change.
Hope dwindles.
Our team
fades in the steam from the showers
under the left-field bleachers.

The myopic umpire yawns through the sixth inning.
He doesn't care who's pinch-hitting,
who's in relief.
But suddenly we do.
Suddenly the game is crucial.
Two on, two out. The three fat women, their hearts at bat,

razz the umpire, curse the visiting coach.

Someone in the boxes calls the ump a jerk.
It's the Baptist minister,
his best sermon ever.
Applause and laughter.
He should run for mayor.
With a crimson nod he returns to his folding chair.
Sudden silence. A bat swishes the air.

Below the stands the ballplayers shrug, their sweat
evaporating.
Somebody snaps the catcher's jockstrap.
In the parking lot his blonde wife
lights discreet cigarettes
and talks of feeling
tired and pregnant.

The fattest woman says she hates these umpires,
says she'll buy the beer.
I dream of nights like this.

Why I Love Baseball

Working my hand into one of those stiff
four-fingered gloves designed for
second basemen, I wonder why
even before the strike, so many people
turned against baseball,
favoring the quick kill,
raw meat, cracked bones, and twisted
ligaments of football.

We have become impatient.
We have lost our enthusiasm
for the subtle, the elusive,
the comforts of peanuts and
sunflower seeds and the sweet
boredom of a summer afternoon.

When I was about eight,
my brother had a glove like this, a glove
that seemed to harden
in the sun.
Nothing could break it in, and when one
golden afternoon he left it stranded on second,
it never returned,
but he came back a few years down the road
unscathed from Vietnam with a story of how he was
left on second with two out
and the score tied
when the mortars fell on Pleiku.

Another brother I know of
apparently tried to field a Cong grenade,
maybe a basket catch like Willie Mays.
But I don't know how much he loved the game.

Gloves like this one hold the hand steady,
as if Rogers Hornsby himself were
holding your hand firmly to the dirt
for a hot grounder years before the war.
With an old glove like this and a new baseball,
you could start the whole world over.

ABOUT THE AUTHOR

Ron McFarland is Professor of English at the University of Idaho. Though born in Ohio and raised in Florida, he has lived and taught in Idaho since 1970. Named the state's first Writer-in-Residence in 1984, he has authored or edited several scholarly studies, including two volumes in the Confluence American Authors Series, *James Welch* and *Norman Maclean*, three pamphlets in the Western Writers Series, and *The Villanelle: The Evolution of a Poetic Form*. He lives with his wife, Elsie, in Moscow. *Stranger in Town* is McFarland's fifth collection of poems.